Animals in My Backyard
BALD EAGLES

Pamela McDowell

AV² provides enriched content that supplements and complements this book. Weigl's AV² book strive to create inspired learning and engage young minds in a total learning experience.

Your AV² Media Enhanced books come alive with...

Audio
Listen to sections of the book read aloud.

Video
Watch informative video clips.

Embedded Weblinks
Gain additional information for research.

Try This!
Complete activities and hands-on experiments.

Key Words
Study vocabulary, and complete a matching word activity.

Quizzes
Test your knowledge.

Slide Show
View images and captions, and prepare a presentation.

... and much, much more!

Go to **www.av2books.com**, and enter this book's unique code.

BOOK CODE

N499950

AV² by Weigl brings you media enhanced books that support active learning.

Published by AV² by Weigl.
350 5th Avenue, 59th Floor, New York, NY 10118
Website: www.av2books.com   www.weigl.com

Library of Congress Cataloging-in-Publication Data

McDowell, Pamela.
 Bald eagles / Pamela McDowell.
    p. cm. -- (Animals in my backyard)
 Includes bibliographical references and index.
 ISBN 978-1-61913-268-9 (hard cover : alk. paper) -- ISBN 978-1-61913-272-6 (soft cover : alk. paper)
 1. Bald eagles--Juvenile literature. I. Title.
 QL696.F32M355 2013
 598.9'42--dc23
                            2011050248

Printed in the United States of America in North Mankato, Minnesota
1 2 3 4 5 6 7 8 9 0 16 15 14 13 12

022012
WEP020212

Project Coordinator: Aaron Carr   Art Director: Terry Paulhus

Weigl acknowledges Getty Images as the primary image supplier for this title.

Animals in My Backyard

BALD EAGLES

CONTENTS

Meet the bald eagle.

He has white feathers on his head.
Dark brown feathers cover his body.

He lives with his family
when he is young.

When he is young, his mother
and father feed him.

He can fly with his long wings.

With his long wings, he can fly as high as an airplane.

Each of his feet has four sharp claws.

Four sharp claws help him hold on to his food.

He sees with two large eyes.

With two large eyes,
he can see food from high in the sky.

He eats with his strong beak.

With his strong beak, he eats small animals and fish.

He lives near water.

Near water, he can find fish to eat.

17

He makes his nest up high in a tree.

Up high in a tree,
his nest is away from danger.

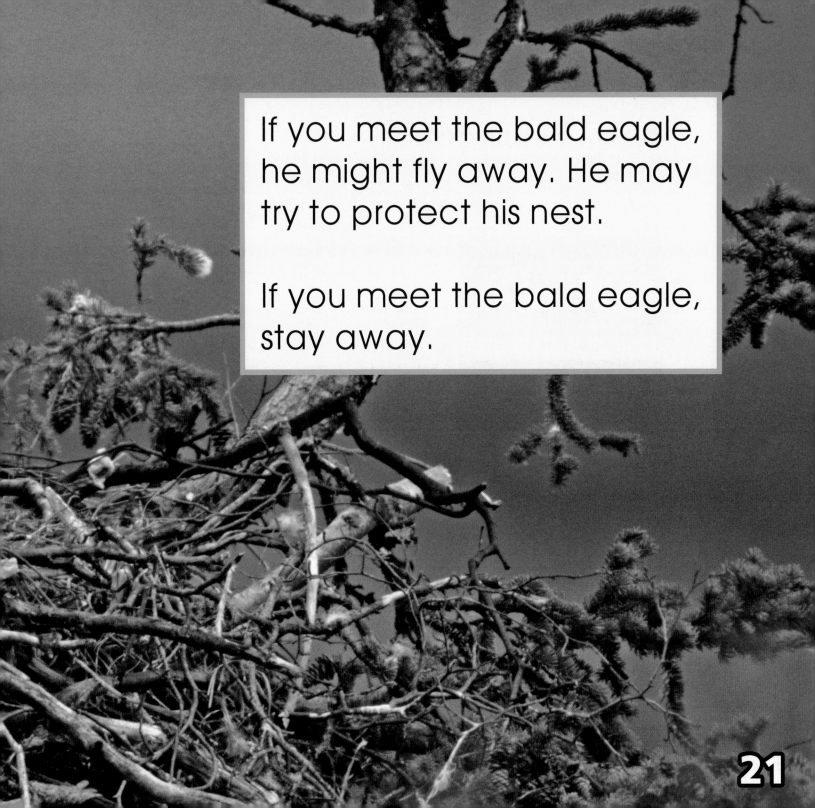

If you meet the bald eagle, he might fly away. He may try to protect his nest.

If you meet the bald eagle, stay away.

BALD EAGLE FACTS

These pages provide more detail about the interesting facts found in the book. They are intended to be used by adults as a learning support to help young readers round out their knowledge of each animal featured in the Animals in My Backyard series.

Pages 4–5

The bald eagle is a bird. It has white feathers on its head. The bald eagle is one of the largest birds of prey. These birds hunt other animals, such as rabbits, turtles, and ducks, for food. Eagles are found all over the world. The bald eagle was declared the national bird of the United States in 1782. An adult eagle has about 7,200 feathers.

Pages 6–7

A baby bald eagle lives with its family. Baby eagles hatch from eggs. They are called chicks. When they get older and larger, they are called eaglets. Eagle parents take turns bringing food to their babies in the nest. At five months, eagles are almost fully grown. They weigh 6.5 to 14 pounds (3 to 6.5 kilograms), about the size of a house cat.

Pages 8–9

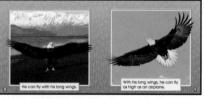

Bald eagles have long wings. An eagle's wingspan is 6 to 8 feet (1.8 to 2.4 meters). This is more than the height of a tall man. Eagles can fly 30 miles (50 kilometres) per hour. They may dive for prey at up to 100 miles (160 km) per hour. Eagles use their powerful wings to soar at heights up to 10,000 feet (3,048 m).

Pages 10–11

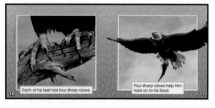

Bald eagles have sharp claws. An eagle's claws, called talons, help the eagle catch its food. The talons are rough, which helps the eagle hold on to slippery prey. An eagle's talons can exert a force of 1,000 pounds per square inch (70 kilograms per square centimeter). This is four times more powerful than the bite of a German shepherd dog.

Pages 12–13

Bald eagles have large eyes. This helps them spot their prey from high in the sky. Sharp vision makes the eagle an excellent hunter. Eagles can see a fish or a rabbit from about 1 mile (1.6 km) away. They can see clearly during the day, but not at night. Eagles see in color, just like humans.

Pages 14–15

Bald eagles have strong beaks. Eagles do not have teeth. An eagle rips its food into pieces with its powerful beak. The hooked end of the beak helps the eagle tear its food. A bald eagle's beak, feathers, and talons are made of keratin. This is the same material that makes up human fingernails.

Pages 16–17

Bald eagles usually live near water. Eagles live in forests, mountains, deserts, and farmland. They build their nests near lakes, rivers, or oceans, where they can find food. They may migrate more than 2,000 miles (3,200 km) in the winter to find warmer weather. Bald eagles return to their nests each spring to raise their young.

Pages 18–19

Bald eagles make their nest high up in trees. An eagle's nest is called an aerie. Male and female eagles build the nest together using sticks, grass, and feathers. The average aerie is about the size of a bathtub. An aerie can weigh as much as a small car. The largest aerie on record weighed more than 4,000 pounds (1,814 kg).

Pages 20–21

Bald eagles are often found in parks and natural areas. A mother eagle is very protective of her eaglets. She will attack raccoons, people, and other birds that get too close to her nest. Bald eagles do not have any natural predators, but they may be killed by other animals that find the eagle's aerie.

WORD LIST

Research has shown that as much as 65 percent of all written material published in English is made up of 300 words. These 300 words cannot be taught using pictures or learned by sounding them out. They must be recognized by sight. This book contains 51 common sight words to help young readers improve their reading fluency and comprehension. This book also teaches young readers several important content words. These words are paired with pictures to aid in learning and improve understanding.

Page	Sight Words First Appearance
4	the
5	has, he, head, his, on, white
6	and, family, father, him, is, lives, mother, when, with, young
8	can, long
9	an, as, high
10	each, feet, four, of
11	food, help, to
12	eyes, large, sees, two
13	from, in
14	eats
15	animals, small
17	find, near, water
18	a, makes, tree, up
19	away
21	if, may, might, try, you

Page	Content Words First Appearance
4	bald eagle
5	body, feathers
8	wings
9	airplane
10	claws
13	sky
14	beak
15	fish
18	nest
19	danger

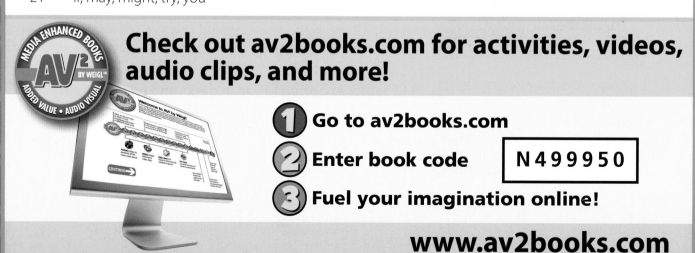